PASSWORD
LOG BOOK

THIS BOOK BELONGS TO:

NAME: _____

PHONE: _____

ADDRESS: _____

_____

INDEX

WEBSITE	PAGE

INDEX

WEBSITE	PAGE

INDEX

WEBSITE	PAGE

INDEX

WEBSITE	PAGE

INDEX

WEBSITE	PAGE

INDEX

WEBSITE	PAGE

INDEX

WEBSITE	PAGE

INDEX

WEBSITE	PAGE

INDEX

WEBSITE	PAGE

INDEX

WEBSITE	PAGE

EMAIL ACCOUNTS

EMAIL	
PASSWORD	
SECURITY ANSWERS	
NOTES	

EMAIL	
PASSWORD	
SECURITY ANSWERS	
NOTES	

EMAIL	
PASSWORD	
SECURITY ANSWERS	
NOTES	

1

EMAIL ACCOUNTS

EMAIL	
PASSWORD	
SECURITY ANSWERS	
NOTES	

EMAIL	
PASSWORD	
SECURITY ANSWERS	
NOTES	

EMAIL	
PASSWORD	
SECURITY ANSWERS	
NOTES	

EMAIL ACCOUNTS

EMAIL	
PASSWORD	
SECURITY ANSWERS	
NOTES	

EMAIL	
PASSWORD	
SECURITY ANSWERS	
NOTES	

EMAIL	
PASSWORD	
SECURITY ANSWERS	
NOTES	

3

SOFTWARE LICENSES

SOFTWARE	
LICENSE NUMBER	
USERNAME	
PASSWORD	
NOTES	

SOFTWARE	
LICENSE NUMBER	
USERNAME	
PASSWORD	
NOTES	

SOFTWARE	
LICENSE NUMBER	
USERNAME	
PASSWORD	
NOTES	

4

SOFTWARE LICENSES

SOFTWARE	
LICENSE NUMBER	
USERNAME	
PASSWORD	
NOTES	

SOFTWARE	
LICENSE NUMBER	
USERNAME	
PASSWORD	
NOTES	

SOFTWARE	
LICENSE NUMBER	
USERNAME	
PASSWORD	
NOTES	

5

SOFTWARE LICENSES

SOFTWARE	
LICENSE NUMBER	
USERNAME	
PASSWORD	
NOTES	

SOFTWARE	
LICENSE NUMBER	
USERNAME	
PASSWORD	
NOTES	

SOFTWARE	
LICENSE NUMBER	
USERNAME	
PASSWORD	
NOTES	

SOFTWARE LICENSES

SOFTWARE	
LICENSE NUMBER	
USERNAME	
PASSWORD	
NOTES	

SOFTWARE	
LICENSE NUMBER	
USERNAME	
PASSWORD	
NOTES	

SOFTWARE	
LICENSE NUMBER	
USERNAME	
PASSWORD	
NOTES	

SOFTWARE LICENSES

SOFTWARE	
LICENSE NUMBER	
USERNAME	
PASSWORD	
NOTES	

SOFTWARE	
LICENSE NUMBER	
USERNAME	
PASSWORD	
NOTES	

SOFTWARE	
LICENSE NUMBER	
USERNAME	
PASSWORD	
NOTES	

8

Internet Information

SITE	
🌐 WEBSITE	
👤 USERNAME	
🔒 PASSWORD	
📃 NOTES	

SITE	
🌐 WEBSITE	
👤 USERNAME	
🔒 PASSWORD	
📃 NOTES	

SITE	
🌐 WEBSITE	
👤 USERNAME	
🔒 PASSWORD	
📃 NOTES	

Internet Information

SITE	
🌐 WEBSITE	
👤 USERNAME	
🔒 PASSWORD	
📝 NOTES	

SITE	
🌐 WEBSITE	
👤 USERNAME	
🔒 PASSWORD	
📝 NOTES	

SITE	
🌐 WEBSITE	
👤 USERNAME	
🔒 PASSWORD	
📝 NOTES	

Internet Information

SITE	
🌐 WEBSITE	
👤 USERNAME	
🔒 PASSWORD	
🗐 NOTES	

SITE	
🌐 WEBSITE	
👤 USERNAME	
🔒 PASSWORD	
🗐 NOTES	

SITE	
🌐 WEBSITE	
👤 USERNAME	
🔒 PASSWORD	
🗐 NOTES	

Internet Information

SITE	
🌐 WEBSITE	
👤 USERNAME	
🔒 PASSWORD	
📧 NOTES	

SITE	
🌐 WEBSITE	
👤 USERNAME	
🔒 PASSWORD	
📧 NOTES	

SITE	
🌐 WEBSITE	
👤 USERNAME	
🔒 PASSWORD	
📧 NOTES	

B Internet Information

SITE	
🌐 WEBSITE	
👤 USERNAME	
🔒 PASSWORD	
🗐 NOTES	

SITE	
🌐 WEBSITE	
👤 USERNAME	
🔒 PASSWORD	
🗐 NOTES	

SITE	
🌐 WEBSITE	
👤 USERNAME	
🔒 PASSWORD	
🗐 NOTES	

SITE	
🌐 WEBSITE	
👤 USERNAME	
🔒 PASSWORD	
🗐 NOTES	

SITE	
🌐 WEBSITE	
👤 USERNAME	
🔒 PASSWORD	
🗐 NOTES	

SITE	
🌐 WEBSITE	
👤 USERNAME	
🔒 PASSWORD	
🗐 NOTES	

C Internet Information

SITE	
🌐 WEBSITE	
👤 USERNAME	
🔒 PASSWORD	
🗐 NOTES	

SITE	
🌐 WEBSITE	
👤 USERNAME	
🔒 PASSWORD	
🗐 NOTES	

SITE	
🌐 WEBSITE	
👤 USERNAME	
🔒 PASSWORD	
🗐 NOTES	

SITE	
🌐 WEBSITE	
👤 USERNAME	
🔒 PASSWORD	
📧 NOTES	

SITE	
🌐 WEBSITE	
👤 USERNAME	
🔒 PASSWORD	
📧 NOTES	

SITE	
🌐 WEBSITE	
👤 USERNAME	
🔒 PASSWORD	
📧 NOTES	

C Internet Information

SITE	
🌐 WEBSITE	
👤 USERNAME	
🔒 PASSWORD	
📋 NOTES	

SITE	
🌐 WEBSITE	
👤 USERNAME	
🔒 PASSWORD	
📋 NOTES	

SITE	
🌐 WEBSITE	
👤 USERNAME	
🔒 PASSWORD	
📋 NOTES	

SITE	
🌐 WEBSITE	
👤 USERNAME	
🔒 PASSWORD	
📧 NOTES	

SITE	
🌐 WEBSITE	
👤 USERNAME	
🔒 PASSWORD	
📧 NOTES	

SITE	
🌐 WEBSITE	
👤 USERNAME	
🔒 PASSWORD	
📧 NOTES	

D Internet Information

SITE	
🌐 WEBSITE	
👤 USERNAME	
🔒 PASSWORD	
📇 NOTES	

SITE	
🌐 WEBSITE	
👤 USERNAME	
🔒 PASSWORD	
📇 NOTES	

SITE	
🌐 WEBSITE	
👤 USERNAME	
🔒 PASSWORD	
📇 NOTES	

Internet Information

SITE	
🌐 WEBSITE	
👤 USERNAME	
🔒 PASSWORD	
📝 NOTES	

SITE	
🌐 WEBSITE	
👤 USERNAME	
🔒 PASSWORD	
📝 NOTES	

SITE	
🌐 WEBSITE	
👤 USERNAME	
🔒 PASSWORD	
📝 NOTES	

Internet Information

SITE	
🌐 WEBSITE	
👤 USERNAME	
🔒 PASSWORD	
📝 NOTES	

SITE	
🌐 WEBSITE	
👤 USERNAME	
🔒 PASSWORD	
📝 NOTES	

SITE	
🌐 WEBSITE	
👤 USERNAME	
🔒 PASSWORD	
📝 NOTES	

SITE	
🌐 WEBSITE	
👤 USERNAME	
🔒 PASSWORD	
🗐 NOTES	

SITE	
🌐 WEBSITE	
👤 USERNAME	
🔒 PASSWORD	
🗐 NOTES	

SITE	
🌐 WEBSITE	
👤 USERNAME	
🔒 PASSWORD	
🗐 NOTES	

Internet Information

SITE	
🌐 WEBSITE	
👤 USERNAME	
🔒 PASSWORD	
🗐 NOTES	

SITE	
🌐 WEBSITE	
👤 USERNAME	
🔒 PASSWORD	
🗐 NOTES	

SITE	
🌐 WEBSITE	
👤 USERNAME	
🔒 PASSWORD	
🗐 NOTES	

Internet Information

SITE	
🌐 WEBSITE	
👤 USERNAME	
🔒 PASSWORD	
🗨 NOTES	

SITE	
🌐 WEBSITE	
👤 USERNAME	
🔒 PASSWORD	
🗨 NOTES	

SITE	
🌐 WEBSITE	
👤 USERNAME	
🔒 PASSWORD	
🗨 NOTES	

24

SITE	
🌐 WEBSITE	
👤 USERNAME	
🔒 PASSWORD	
🗨 NOTES	

SITE	
🌐 WEBSITE	
👤 USERNAME	
🔒 PASSWORD	
🗨 NOTES	

SITE	
🌐 WEBSITE	
👤 USERNAME	
🔒 PASSWORD	
🗨 NOTES	

SITE	
🌐 WEBSITE	
👤 USERNAME	
🔒 PASSWORD	
📋 NOTES	

SITE	
🌐 WEBSITE	
👤 USERNAME	
🔒 PASSWORD	
📋 NOTES	

SITE	
🌐 WEBSITE	
👤 USERNAME	
🔒 PASSWORD	
📋 NOTES	

SITE	
🌐 WEBSITE	
👤 USERNAME	
🔒 PASSWORD	
🗐 NOTES	

SITE	
🌐 WEBSITE	
👤 USERNAME	
🔒 PASSWORD	
🗐 NOTES	

SITE	
🌐 WEBSITE	
👤 USERNAME	
🔒 PASSWORD	
🗐 NOTES	

Internet Information

SITE	
🌐 WEBSITE	
👤 USERNAME	
🔒 PASSWORD	
📑 NOTES	

SITE	
🌐 WEBSITE	
👤 USERNAME	
🔒 PASSWORD	
📑 NOTES	

SITE	
🌐 WEBSITE	
👤 USERNAME	
🔒 PASSWORD	
📑 NOTES	

SITE	
🌐 WEBSITE	
👤 USERNAME	
🔒 PASSWORD	
📋 NOTES	

SITE	
🌐 WEBSITE	
👤 USERNAME	
🔒 PASSWORD	
📋 NOTES	

SITE	
🌐 WEBSITE	
👤 USERNAME	
🔒 PASSWORD	
📋 NOTES	

SITE	
🌐 WEBSITE	
👤 USERNAME	
🔒 PASSWORD	
🗐 NOTES	

SITE	
🌐 WEBSITE	
👤 USERNAME	
🔒 PASSWORD	
🗐 NOTES	

SITE	
🌐 WEBSITE	
👤 USERNAME	
🔒 PASSWORD	
🗐 NOTES	

H Internet Information

SITE	
🌐 WEBSITE	
👤 USERNAME	
🔒 PASSWORD	
🗐 NOTES	

SITE	
🌐 WEBSITE	
👤 USERNAME	
🔒 PASSWORD	
🗐 NOTES	

SITE	
🌐 WEBSITE	
👤 USERNAME	
🔒 PASSWORD	
🗐 NOTES	

SITE	
WEBSITE	
USERNAME	
PASSWORD	
NOTES	

SITE	
WEBSITE	
USERNAME	
PASSWORD	
NOTES	

SITE	
WEBSITE	
USERNAME	
PASSWORD	
NOTES	

SITE	
🌐 WEBSITE	
👤 USERNAME	
🔒 PASSWORD	
🗨 NOTES	

SITE	
🌐 WEBSITE	
👤 USERNAME	
🔒 PASSWORD	
🗨 NOTES	

SITE	
🌐 WEBSITE	
👤 USERNAME	
🔒 PASSWORD	
🗨 NOTES	

SITE	
🌐 WEBSITE	
👤 USERNAME	
🔒 PASSWORD	
📋 NOTES	

SITE	
🌐 WEBSITE	
👤 USERNAME	
🔒 PASSWORD	
📋 NOTES	

SITE	
🌐 WEBSITE	
👤 USERNAME	
🔒 PASSWORD	
📋 NOTES	

Internet Information

SITE	
🌐 WEBSITE	
👤 USERNAME	
🔒 PASSWORD	
🗄 NOTES	

SITE	
🌐 WEBSITE	
👤 USERNAME	
🔒 PASSWORD	
🗄 NOTES	

SITE	
🌐 WEBSITE	
👤 USERNAME	
🔒 PASSWORD	
🗄 NOTES	

SITE	
🌐 WEBSITE	
👤 USERNAME	
🔒 PASSWORD	
🖹 NOTES	

SITE	
🌐 WEBSITE	
👤 USERNAME	
🔒 PASSWORD	
🖹 NOTES	

SITE	
🌐 WEBSITE	
👤 USERNAME	
🔒 PASSWORD	
🖹 NOTES	

J Internet Information

SITE	
🌐 WEBSITE	
👤 USERNAME	
🔒 PASSWORD	
📝 NOTES	

SITE	
🌐 WEBSITE	
👤 USERNAME	
🔒 PASSWORD	
📝 NOTES	

SITE	
🌐 WEBSITE	
👤 USERNAME	
🔒 PASSWORD	
📝 NOTES	

SITE	
🌐 WEBSITE	
👤 USERNAME	
🔒 PASSWORD	
📇 NOTES	

SITE	
🌐 WEBSITE	
👤 USERNAME	
🔒 PASSWORD	
📇 NOTES	

SITE	
🌐 WEBSITE	
👤 USERNAME	
🔒 PASSWORD	
📇 NOTES	

Internet Information

SITE	
WEBSITE	
USERNAME	
PASSWORD	
NOTES	

SITE	
WEBSITE	
USERNAME	
PASSWORD	
NOTES	

SITE	
WEBSITE	
USERNAME	
PASSWORD	
NOTES	

39

SITE	
🌐 WEBSITE	
👤 USERNAME	
🔒 PASSWORD	
📑 NOTES	

SITE	
🌐 WEBSITE	
👤 USERNAME	
🔒 PASSWORD	
📑 NOTES	

SITE	
🌐 WEBSITE	
👤 USERNAME	
🔒 PASSWORD	
📑 NOTES	

Internet Information

SITE	
🌐 WEBSITE	
👤 USERNAME	
🔒 PASSWORD	
📝 NOTES	

SITE	
🌐 WEBSITE	
👤 USERNAME	
🔒 PASSWORD	
📝 NOTES	

SITE	
🌐 WEBSITE	
👤 USERNAME	
🔒 PASSWORD	
📝 NOTES	

41

Internet Information

SITE	
🌐 WEBSITE	
👤 USERNAME	
🔒 PASSWORD	
🗐 NOTES	

SITE	
🌐 WEBSITE	
👤 USERNAME	
🔒 PASSWORD	
🗐 NOTES	

SITE	
🌐 WEBSITE	
👤 USERNAME	
🔒 PASSWORD	
🗐 NOTES	

SITE	
🌐 WEBSITE	
👤 USERNAME	
🔒 PASSWORD	
🗎 NOTES	

SITE	
🌐 WEBSITE	
👤 USERNAME	
🔒 PASSWORD	
🗎 NOTES	

SITE	
🌐 WEBSITE	
👤 USERNAME	
🔒 PASSWORD	
🗎 NOTES	

Internet Information

SITE	
🌐 WEBSITE	
👤 USERNAME	
🔒 PASSWORD	
🗨 NOTES	

SITE	
🌐 WEBSITE	
👤 USERNAME	
🔒 PASSWORD	
🗨 NOTES	

SITE	
🌐 WEBSITE	
👤 USERNAME	
🔒 PASSWORD	
🗨 NOTES	

44

M Internet Information

SITE	
🌐 WEBSITE	
👤 USERNAME	
🔒 PASSWORD	
🗐 NOTES	

SITE	
🌐 WEBSITE	
👤 USERNAME	
🔒 PASSWORD	
🗐 NOTES	

SITE	
🌐 WEBSITE	
👤 USERNAME	
🔒 PASSWORD	
🗐 NOTES	

Internet Information

SITE	
🌐 WEBSITE	
👤 USERNAME	
🔒 PASSWORD	
📋 NOTES	

SITE	
🌐 WEBSITE	
👤 USERNAME	
🔒 PASSWORD	
📋 NOTES	

SITE	
🌐 WEBSITE	
👤 USERNAME	
🔒 PASSWORD	
📋 NOTES	

SITE	
🌐 WEBSITE	
👤 USERNAME	
🔒 PASSWORD	
🗐 NOTES	

SITE	
🌐 WEBSITE	
👤 USERNAME	
🔒 PASSWORD	
🗐 NOTES	

SITE	
🌐 WEBSITE	
👤 USERNAME	
🔒 PASSWORD	
🗐 NOTES	

SITE	
🌐 WEBSITE	
👤 USERNAME	
🔒 PASSWORD	
📑 NOTES	

SITE	
🌐 WEBSITE	
👤 USERNAME	
🔒 PASSWORD	
📑 NOTES	

SITE	
🌐 WEBSITE	
👤 USERNAME	
🔒 PASSWORD	
📑 NOTES	

N Internet Information

SITE	
🌐 WEBSITE	
👤 USERNAME	
🔒 PASSWORD	
📋 NOTES	

SITE	
🌐 WEBSITE	
👤 USERNAME	
🔒 PASSWORD	
📋 NOTES	

SITE	
🌐 WEBSITE	
👤 USERNAME	
🔒 PASSWORD	
📋 NOTES	

Internet Information

SITE	
🌐 WEBSITE	
👤 USERNAME	
🔒 PASSWORD	
📑 NOTES	

SITE	
🌐 WEBSITE	
👤 USERNAME	
🔒 PASSWORD	
📑 NOTES	

SITE	
🌐 WEBSITE	
👤 USERNAME	
🔒 PASSWORD	
📑 NOTES	

Internet Information

SITE	
WEBSITE	
USERNAME	
PASSWORD	
NOTES	

SITE	
WEBSITE	
USERNAME	
PASSWORD	
NOTES	

SITE	
WEBSITE	
USERNAME	
PASSWORD	
NOTES	

Internet Information

SITE	
🌐 WEBSITE	
👤 USERNAME	
🔒 PASSWORD	
📋 NOTES	

SITE	
🌐 WEBSITE	
👤 USERNAME	
🔒 PASSWORD	
📋 NOTES	

SITE	
🌐 WEBSITE	
👤 USERNAME	
🔒 PASSWORD	
📋 NOTES	

O Internet Information

SITE	
🌐 WEBSITE	
👤 USERNAME	
🔒 PASSWORD	
📋 NOTES	

SITE	
🌐 WEBSITE	
👤 USERNAME	
🔒 PASSWORD	
📋 NOTES	

SITE	
🌐 WEBSITE	
👤 USERNAME	
🔒 PASSWORD	
📋 NOTES	

53

SITE	
🌐 WEBSITE	
👤 USERNAME	
🔒 PASSWORD	
📋 NOTES	

SITE	
🌐 WEBSITE	
👤 USERNAME	
🔒 PASSWORD	
📋 NOTES	

SITE	
🌐 WEBSITE	
👤 USERNAME	
🔒 PASSWORD	
📋 NOTES	

P Internet Information

SITE	
WEBSITE	
USERNAME	
PASSWORD	
NOTES	

SITE	
WEBSITE	
USERNAME	
PASSWORD	
NOTES	

SITE	
WEBSITE	
USERNAME	
PASSWORD	
NOTES	

55

Internet Information

SITE	
🌐 WEBSITE	
👤 USERNAME	
🔒 PASSWORD	
🗨 NOTES	

SITE	
🌐 WEBSITE	
👤 USERNAME	
🔒 PASSWORD	
🗨 NOTES	

SITE	
🌐 WEBSITE	
👤 USERNAME	
🔒 PASSWORD	
🗨 NOTES	

SITE	
🌐 WEBSITE	
👤 USERNAME	
🔒 PASSWORD	
📝 NOTES	

SITE	
🌐 WEBSITE	
👤 USERNAME	
🔒 PASSWORD	
📝 NOTES	

SITE	
🌐 WEBSITE	
👤 USERNAME	
🔒 PASSWORD	
📝 NOTES	

SITE	
🌐 WEBSITE	
👤 USERNAME	
🔒 PASSWORD	
📧 NOTES	

SITE	
🌐 WEBSITE	
👤 USERNAME	
🔒 PASSWORD	
📧 NOTES	

SITE	
🌐 WEBSITE	
👤 USERNAME	
🔒 PASSWORD	
📧 NOTES	

SITE	
WEBSITE	
USERNAME	
PASSWORD	
NOTES	

SITE	
WEBSITE	
USERNAME	
PASSWORD	
NOTES	

SITE	
WEBSITE	
USERNAME	
PASSWORD	
NOTES	

Internet Information

SITE	
🌐 WEBSITE	
👤 USERNAME	
🔒 PASSWORD	
🗨 NOTES	

SITE	
🌐 WEBSITE	
👤 USERNAME	
🔒 PASSWORD	
🗨 NOTES	

SITE	
🌐 WEBSITE	
👤 USERNAME	
🔒 PASSWORD	
🗨 NOTES	

Internet Information

SITE	
🌐 WEBSITE	
👤 USERNAME	
🔒 PASSWORD	
📑 NOTES	

SITE	
🌐 WEBSITE	
👤 USERNAME	
🔒 PASSWORD	
📑 NOTES	

SITE	
🌐 WEBSITE	
👤 USERNAME	
🔒 PASSWORD	
📑 NOTES	

Internet Information

SITE	
🌐 WEBSITE	
👤 USERNAME	
🔒 PASSWORD	
🗐 NOTES	

SITE	
🌐 WEBSITE	
👤 USERNAME	
🔒 PASSWORD	
🗐 NOTES	

SITE	
🌐 WEBSITE	
👤 USERNAME	
🔒 PASSWORD	
🗐 NOTES	

SITE	
✪ WEBSITE	
👤 USERNAME	
🔒 PASSWORD	
📇 NOTES	

SITE	
✪ WEBSITE	
👤 USERNAME	
🔒 PASSWORD	
📇 NOTES	

SITE	
✪ WEBSITE	
👤 USERNAME	
🔒 PASSWORD	
📇 NOTES	

SITE	
🌐 WEBSITE	
👤 USERNAME	
🔒 PASSWORD	
🗨 NOTES	

SITE	
🌐 WEBSITE	
👤 USERNAME	
🔒 PASSWORD	
🗨 NOTES	

SITE	
🌐 WEBSITE	
👤 USERNAME	
🔒 PASSWORD	
🗨 NOTES	

S **Internet Information**

SITE	
🌐 WEBSITE	
👤 USERNAME	
🔒 PASSWORD	
🗐 NOTES	

SITE	
🌐 WEBSITE	
👤 USERNAME	
🔒 PASSWORD	
🗐 NOTES	

SITE	
🌐 WEBSITE	
👤 USERNAME	
🔒 PASSWORD	
🗐 NOTES	

Internet Information

SITE	
🌐 WEBSITE	
👤 USERNAME	
🔒 PASSWORD	
📇 NOTES	

SITE	
🌐 WEBSITE	
👤 USERNAME	
🔒 PASSWORD	
📇 NOTES	

SITE	
🌐 WEBSITE	
👤 USERNAME	
🔒 PASSWORD	
📇 NOTES	

T Internet Information

SITE	
🌐 WEBSITE	
👤 USERNAME	
🔒 PASSWORD	
🗐 NOTES	

SITE	
🌐 WEBSITE	
👤 USERNAME	
🔒 PASSWORD	
🗐 NOTES	

SITE	
🌐 WEBSITE	
👤 USERNAME	
🔒 PASSWORD	
🗐 NOTES	

Internet Information

SITE	
🌐 WEBSITE	
👤 USERNAME	
🔒 PASSWORD	
📝 NOTES	

SITE	
🌐 WEBSITE	
👤 USERNAME	
🔒 PASSWORD	
📝 NOTES	

SITE	
🌐 WEBSITE	
👤 USERNAME	
🔒 PASSWORD	
📝 NOTES	

SITE	
🌐 WEBSITE	
👤 USERNAME	
🔒 PASSWORD	
🗐 NOTES	

SITE	
🌐 WEBSITE	
👤 USERNAME	
🔒 PASSWORD	
🗐 NOTES	

SITE	
🌐 WEBSITE	
👤 USERNAME	
🔒 PASSWORD	
🗐 NOTES	

Internet Information

SITE	
🌐 WEBSITE	
👤 USERNAME	
🔒 PASSWORD	
🗐 NOTES	

SITE	
🌐 WEBSITE	
👤 USERNAME	
🔒 PASSWORD	
🗐 NOTES	

SITE	
🌐 WEBSITE	
👤 USERNAME	
🔒 PASSWORD	
🗐 NOTES	

U Internet Information

SITE	
WEBSITE	
USERNAME	
PASSWORD	
NOTES	

SITE	
WEBSITE	
USERNAME	
PASSWORD	
NOTES	

SITE	
WEBSITE	
USERNAME	
PASSWORD	
NOTES	

71

Internet Information

SITE	
🌐 WEBSITE	
👤 USERNAME	
🔒 PASSWORD	
📝 NOTES	

SITE	
🌐 WEBSITE	
👤 USERNAME	
🔒 PASSWORD	
📝 NOTES	

SITE	
🌐 WEBSITE	
👤 USERNAME	
🔒 PASSWORD	
📝 NOTES	

Internet Information

SITE	
🌐 WEBSITE	
👤 USERNAME	
🔒 PASSWORD	
📋 NOTES	

SITE	
🌐 WEBSITE	
👤 USERNAME	
🔒 PASSWORD	
📋 NOTES	

SITE	
🌐 WEBSITE	
👤 USERNAME	
🔒 PASSWORD	
📋 NOTES	

Internet Information

SITE	
🌐 WEBSITE	
👤 USERNAME	
🔒 PASSWORD	
📇 NOTES	

SITE	
🌐 WEBSITE	
👤 USERNAME	
🔒 PASSWORD	
📇 NOTES	

SITE	
🌐 WEBSITE	
👤 USERNAME	
🔒 PASSWORD	
📇 NOTES	

SITE	
🌐 WEBSITE	
👤 USERNAME	
🔒 PASSWORD	
🗐 NOTES	

SITE	
🌐 WEBSITE	
👤 USERNAME	
🔒 PASSWORD	
🗐 NOTES	

SITE	
🌐 WEBSITE	
👤 USERNAME	
🔒 PASSWORD	
🗐 NOTES	

Internet Information

SITE	
🌐 WEBSITE	
👤 USERNAME	
🔒 PASSWORD	
📋 NOTES	

SITE	
🌐 WEBSITE	
👤 USERNAME	
🔒 PASSWORD	
📋 NOTES	

SITE	
🌐 WEBSITE	
👤 USERNAME	
🔒 PASSWORD	
📋 NOTES	

Internet Information

SITE	
🌐 WEBSITE	
👤 USERNAME	
🔒 PASSWORD	
📋 NOTES	

SITE	
🌐 WEBSITE	
👤 USERNAME	
🔒 PASSWORD	
📋 NOTES	

SITE	
🌐 WEBSITE	
👤 USERNAME	
🔒 PASSWORD	
📋 NOTES	

Internet Information

SITE	
🌐 WEBSITE	
👤 USERNAME	
🔒 PASSWORD	
📰 NOTES	

SITE	
🌐 WEBSITE	
👤 USERNAME	
🔒 PASSWORD	
📰 NOTES	

SITE	
🌐 WEBSITE	
👤 USERNAME	
🔒 PASSWORD	
📰 NOTES	

Internet Information

SITE	
🌐 WEBSITE	
👤 USERNAME	
🔒 PASSWORD	
📇 NOTES	

SITE	
🌐 WEBSITE	
👤 USERNAME	
🔒 PASSWORD	
📇 NOTES	

SITE	
🌐 WEBSITE	
👤 USERNAME	
🔒 PASSWORD	
📇 NOTES	

SITE	
🌐 WEBSITE	
👤 USERNAME	
🔒 PASSWORD	
🗨 NOTES	

SITE	
🌐 WEBSITE	
👤 USERNAME	
🔒 PASSWORD	
🗨 NOTES	

SITE	
🌐 WEBSITE	
👤 USERNAME	
🔒 PASSWORD	
🗨 NOTES	

Internet Information

SITE	
🌐 WEBSITE	
👤 USERNAME	
🔒 PASSWORD	
📋 NOTES	

SITE	
🌐 WEBSITE	
👤 USERNAME	
🔒 PASSWORD	
📋 NOTES	

SITE	
🌐 WEBSITE	
👤 USERNAME	
🔒 PASSWORD	
📋 NOTES	

81

Internet Information

SITE	
🌐 WEBSITE	
👤 USERNAME	
🔒 PASSWORD	
📧 NOTES	

SITE	
🌐 WEBSITE	
👤 USERNAME	
🔒 PASSWORD	
📧 NOTES	

SITE	
🌐 WEBSITE	
👤 USERNAME	
🔒 PASSWORD	
📧 NOTES	

Internet Information

SITE	
🌐 WEBSITE	
👤 USERNAME	
🔒 PASSWORD	
📇 NOTES	

SITE	
🌐 WEBSITE	
👤 USERNAME	
🔒 PASSWORD	
📇 NOTES	

SITE	
🌐 WEBSITE	
👤 USERNAME	
🔒 PASSWORD	
📇 NOTES	

Internet Information

SITE	
🌐 WEBSITE	
👤 USERNAME	
🔒 PASSWORD	
📧 NOTES	

SITE	
🌐 WEBSITE	
👤 USERNAME	
🔒 PASSWORD	
📧 NOTES	

SITE	
🌐 WEBSITE	
👤 USERNAME	
🔒 PASSWORD	
📧 NOTES	

Z Internet Information

SITE	
🌐 WEBSITE	
👤 USERNAME	
🔒 PASSWORD	
📝 NOTES	

SITE	
🌐 WEBSITE	
👤 USERNAME	
🔒 PASSWORD	
📝 NOTES	

SITE	
🌐 WEBSITE	
👤 USERNAME	
🔒 PASSWORD	
📝 NOTES	

SITE	
WEBSITE	
USERNAME	
PASSWORD	
NOTES	

SITE	
WEBSITE	
USERNAME	
PASSWORD	
NOTES	

SITE	
WEBSITE	
USERNAME	
PASSWORD	
NOTES	

SITE	
🌐 WEBSITE	
👤 USERNAME	
🔒 PASSWORD	
📄 NOTES	

SITE	
🌐 WEBSITE	
👤 USERNAME	
🔒 PASSWORD	
📄 NOTES	

SITE	
🌐 WEBSITE	
👤 USERNAME	
🔒 PASSWORD	
📄 NOTES	

NOTES

NOTES

NOTES

NOTES

NOTES

NOTES

Made in the USA
Las Vegas, NV
21 December 2021